How Social Anx You Back at Wo

And What to Do About It

By David Leads

Site: http://www.relationshipup.com

Books: http://www.relationshipupbooks.com

Copyright © 2015 Relationship Up. All Rights Reserved.

This book or any portion thereof may not be reproduced in any form without the prior written permission of the publisher, except for the use of brief quotations in a book review.

To contact the publisher, please visit the publisher's website.

Disclaimer

No part of this publication may be reproduced or transmitted in any form or by any means, without prior written permission from the publisher.

While all attempts have been made to verify the information provided in this publication, neither the author, editor, or publisher assume any responsibility for errors, omissions, or contrary interpretations of the subject matter herein. The author, editor, and publisher do not assume and hereby disclaim any liability to any party for any loss, damage, or disruption caused by errors or omissions, whether such errors or omissions result from negligence, accident, or any other cause.

This book is for informational purposes only. The views expressed are those of the author, editor, and publisher alone, and should not be taken as expert instruction or commands. This book is not a substitution for professional, medical, or expert advice and information.

The reader is solely responsible for his or her own actions.

The author, editor, and publisher assume no responsibility or liability whatsoever for any and all consequential actions taken, whether monetary, legal, or otherwise, by any and all readers of the materials provided.

Your Free Gift

In 1938, 268 Harvard undergraduate men were followed for 75 years in what became one of the longest longitudinal studies of human development. Its purpose was to figure out what exactly contributed towards a good life.

Harvard Professor George Vaillant directed this study for more than three decades. Over and over again in his research he reiterated the power of relationships. In March 2008, he was interviewed and asked what he had learned from the study. His response –

> "That the only thing that really matters in life are your relationships to other people."

We believe your relationships are truly the most important thing in your life too. And in addition to the relationships you have with others, the relationship you have with yourself is also important. If you don't have a good relationship with yourself, it's hard to have good relationships with others. Everything we do at Relationship Up revolves around these two types of relationships you have – that with yourself and that with others.

The purpose of this book and all of our other publications is to help you improve your relationships so you can live a happier life. However, one thing that can easily get in the way of a good relationship is conflict.

Conflict between people happens all the time – and it's a major issue that disrupts relationships. Learning to prevent conflict and manage it when it arises is a skill you can learn that will improve your relationships across the board.

There are small tips, tactics, and strategies you can use to get better at keeping the peace between yourself and others. We compiled these in a book for you – *The 37 Best Ways to End Conflict in Your Relationships*.

In this book you'll learn the *what* and the *why* of each of the 37 ways to end a conflict. Even if you just implement one new way to end conflict you'll make lasting positive changes to the way you deal with other people.

As a way of saying *thank you* for your purchase, we're giving you this free book – exclusive to our readers.

Please visit www.relationshipup.com to receive your free gift.

The 37 Best Ways to End Conflict in Your Relationships

DAVID LEADS

What is Relationship Up?

There's so much information on the Internet about relationships, how to get along with people, and how to be a better person. Just doing a quick Google search on a personal problem you're currently having can leave you overwhelmed with the number of sources out there. We asked a lot of people where they went online for relationship help and advice. A lot of the responses we received indicated that people **didn't** use the Internet to find help with relationships. Instead they would go to their family, friends, clergy member, or spouse.

Why not look online for relationship advice? All the other information in the world is online, so why leave out relationships?

The response was – nothing out there is trustworthy. The sites people did frequent were *tabloid-like* in their presentation and information. Pretty much talking about sex 24/7 while ignoring a host of other common problems people have. Those sites seem to be more focused on clicks than on genuinely helping people. Also, people said that relationship problems are inherently unique, with each person facing a different problem in different individual circumstances. While this is true, there are principles and things people can do that can help them in any situation. Though our situations and life perspectives are always unique, others have experienced the same underlying issues before, and we can learn how others have done it in the past to increase our own wellbeing.

Relationship Up started in order to filter through all of this noise. We're interested in the principles that work, and we're even more interested in what to do and how to do it. We publish books on specific relationship issues with the intention that they are easy to understand, quick reads, and full of actionable and valuable information.

Improving a character trait, or improving any relationship, takes a tremendous amount of time, effort, patience, and dedication. Some say that working on yourself takes a lifetime of work! The information and books we publish are meant to serve as your guide as you make the necessary changes in your life to be a better person. Stay the course and stick with your desire to improve your life. We support you, we're proud of you, and we're rooting for your success.

Everything we write about relates to issues between people, or issues you have with yourself. We hope that we can help people improve their relationships and thus add meaning to their lives.

We're just getting started so please leave a review for this book and let us know what you think, how we can improve, and how we can do better.

Visit us at http://www.relationshipup.com or email us at info@relationshipup.com

Table of Contents

Your Free Gift

What is Relationship Up?

Introduction

Part 1 – Understanding Social Anxiety

    What Is Social Anxiety

    How Social Anxiety Affects Your Work Life

    Most Common Workplace Anxieties

    General Advice to Keep Social Anxiety in Check

Part 2 - Coping with Social Anxiety in Your Professional Life

    How to Cope With Job Interview Anxiety

    How to Successfully Handle Meetings

    Networking with Social Anxiety

    How to Calmly Deal with Clients

    How to Manage Office Crushes

    How to Ask for a Promotion/Raise

[Quick Relaxation Techniques That Work](#)

[Conclusion](#)

[Stay Connected](#)

[Thank You](#)

[More Books by David Leads](#)

Introduction

Whenever I think back to my first job interview, I can't help but cringe. I was fresh out of college, wearing a poor-tailored suit, feeling like I'm going to pass out right after I shake hands with the hiring manager. That didn't happen, luckily; however, it didn't go very well either. There were a lot of "umms" mixed into the conversation and I was visibly shaking for a large chunk of the interview. All in all, I didn't make a good first impression. And it wasn't because I didn't take the time to prepare. It was because I couldn't contain my anxiety.

I've never been big on social situations, but things got worse around high school. It's not easy to spend your days stressing over the fact that you will do something utterly embarrassing when you're around people. Or that everyone will judge you for every little mistake you make. They will criticize the clothes you're wearing, your posture, your voice, your hair. They will somehow figure out your deepest thoughts and make fun of those as well. Social anxiety was starting to get in the way of my ability to function like a normal human being and enjoy life.

As I grew older, I figured out a few ways to manage my social fears. I was lucky enough to befriend a couple of wonderful people who made me feel comfortable having them around. Who didn't mind spending a night in watching movies and munching on frozen pizza, and didn't feel the need to badger me about my basically nonexistent social life. When it was time to join the workforce though, I knew things would get more difficult.

A workplace generally entails meetings, small talk, and collaboration. All which scared the bejesus out of me. After a bunch of failed interviews, I was completely discouraged. "I should find a job I can perform from home, that involves zero human interaction," I told myself. And then it hit me: I was allowing my anxiety to dictate my career. Never mind my long-term professional goals. I was actually willing to settle for a disappointing gig just because I dreaded being around people. That thought scared me more than any workplace socializing nightmare could; so I decided to push through and find a way to keep my social fears in check, even if that meant getting out of my comfort zone.

Fast forward to today. I'm still struggling with social anxiety, but I've learned to manage it. I can go through an interview all smiles and no hyperventilating. I can speak up during a meeting and entertain my colleagues around the water cooler. It wasn't an easy road, but I feel like I've grown a lot along the way. Most importantly – I figured out that my social anxiety is highly treatable.

One in six workers is experiencing stress, anxiety or depression; with anxiety disorders being the most prevalent mental health problems worldwide. If you are dealing with social anxiety, you're not alone; and you can get better. This book will show you how.

Part 1 – Understanding Social Anxiety

What Is Social Anxiety?

To put it simply, social anxiety or social phobia is the fear of being judged and evaluated negatively by other people. It often leads to feelings of inadequacy, inferiority, embarrassment, humiliation, or even depression. According to The Anxiety and Depression Association of America, about 15 million American adults have social anxiety disorder.

In some cases, symptoms may be so extreme that they disrupt daily life. People with this disorder may have few or no social or romantic relationships, which makes them feel powerless, lonely, and sometimes even ashamed. What's worse, 36 percent of people with social anxiety disorder report symptoms for 10 or more years before seeking professional help.

Social anxiety isn't rational, and most people who suffer from it are aware of this fact. They realize that a large portion of their thoughts make no sense at all. It's actually one of the most frustrating things about the disorder: you know that you're freaking out despite the fact that you have no valid reason to freak out, but you are unable to shut down your emotions.

The disorder comes in many shapes and forms. Some people develop anxiety as a result of a specific event, yet others experience it due to their brain chemistry. Anxiety can even be genetic. Additionally, some people deal with social anxiety all their lives, while others only develop it as a teen or adult. There are no clear rules about the disorder, and everyone experiences it in their own, deeply personal way. However, most people who are suffering from social phobia feel the need to isolate themselves – which can easily lead to a lonely and unfulfilling life.

Social anxiety has certain triggers, the most common example being anxiety over public speaking. Other triggers can include making small talk, eating in front of others, going to a social event, or using public restrooms. Sometimes, even thoughts of interacting with others can cause extreme distress. Being introduced to other people, being teased, or becoming the center of attention also make the list.

For instance, the first time my coworkers decided to celebrate my birthday at the office was horrible, despite of their good intentions. They brought me a cake, gathered in the conference room, and proceeded to sing me *Happy Birthday*. Meanwhile, I was sitting quietly in the middle of the room, feeling everyone's eyes on me, taking deep breaths and doing my best to not run out the door and isolate myself in the bathroom. What was supposed to be a joyful occasion suddenly became a source of extreme stress, and later a painful memory.

People who suffer from social anxiety react in different ways. Rapid breathing, shaky voice, and sweating are the most noticeable signs that someone is panicking. Most commonly, the feelings that accompany social anxiety include fear, nervousness, racing heart, blushing, excessive sweating, dry throat and mouth, trembling, and muscle twitches. Besides being emotionally painful, social phobia can also physically hurt. Panic attacks are linked to chest pains – people who experienced at least one are familiar with the dreaded feeling that your chest is tightening to the point that you can't breathe. Social anxiety can also cause nausea, heart palpitations, insomnia, muscle tension, headaches, or exhaustion. Anxiety is linked to depression as well – these disorders don't always come together, but they are known as common companions. More accurately, one can easily lead to the other. People who are socially anxious can eventually get depressed because they feel like they are unable to successfully interact with others, while depressed people can end up with social anxiety because they spend too much time alone, isolating themselves whenever possible.

Paradoxically, people with social anxiety aren't antisocial. They are often perceived as shy, unfriendly, quiet, and aloof, yes, but they actually want to make friends and be engaged in social activities. Unfortunately though, their disorder holds them back. As much as they would like to appear open and sociable, that awful fear of interaction stands between them and a rich social life. Again, it's extremely frustrating.

When you suffer from social anxiety, the disorder can interfere with your ability to enjoy life. Social phobia makes you a bit *too* aware of what you're doing and how you're acting around others. Instead of feeling good and relaxed out in public, you feel like you're under a microscope and everyone is judging you. You end up paying way too much attention to yourself and worrying about how everyone perceives you.

Excitement is also a rare sensation. While your friends express their enthusiasm over an upcoming event, you can't help but worry that the event will end up crippling you emotionally. You fight with anticipating anxiety for weeks before the big day, and you might even cancel going at the last minute, because you can't deal with your fears anymore.

Social phobia is commonly associated with low self-esteem. When you dread social interactions you hold yourself back, don't take part in conversations as much as you should, and censor yourself because of your fear of being criticized and rejected. You are also hypersensitive to criticism. You can take feedback that was meant to be constructive the wrong way, or feel like you're a failure when someone gives you advice. Your brain is always in defense-mode, and you tend to interpret everything in a negatively skewed way.

As if all the things I've listen above weren't enough, people with social anxiety also tend to be extremely harsh with themselves. When you're social anxious, you often spend your time replaying events in your head and beating yourself up over how you've "failed miserably". You become certain that people noticed your anxiety and judged you because of it. You obsess over past interactions and become overly critical of your behavior and actions. You're sure you made a fool of yourself, even though there's a small chance others even noticed how uncomfortable you truly were. Some socially anxious folks go their entire lives re-living a presumably failed experience, whether we're talking about a public presentation or a bad date. Replaying these low moments of your life over and over again only reinforce your feelings of failure and defeat.

However, the intensity of all these anxious feelings isn't consistent. Some days are good anxiety days, while some are bad. A situation that can feel panic attack inducing on a bad day can become highly manageable on a good day. But, people with social anxiety disorder can learn how to keep their feelings under control. And that's what this book is about.

How Social Anxiety Affects Your Work Life

While social anxiety can affect your personal life, preventing you from developing healthy personal relationships, it can also negatively impact your career. Anxiety can damage your work performance, as well as your relationships with coworkers, clients, and superiors.

While a certain amount of work-related stress can be beneficial, as it can boost your productivity, stress and anxiety don't work well together. A study conducted by the Anxiety and Depression Association of America revealed that 72 percent of people who experience daily stress and anxiety say it interferes with their lives at least moderately, while 40 percent admit that they experience persistent stress or excessive anxiety in their daily lives. Additionally, 28 percent of workers have had an anxiety or panic attack at least once. People who suffer from social anxiety disorder often spend a lot of time unemployed, change jobs frequently, or struggle through anxiety day after day on the job.

A while back, I joined a forum (www.socialanxietysupport.com) meant to offer support for people dealing with social anxiety. A lot of the users were complaining about how difficult it is to keep social anxiety in check while at the job, feeling insecure and inadequate for the majority of the work day.

One user's account of their struggles really struck a chord with me:

"For the past three weeks I've been working full-time at a retail outlet on a work experience program type thing. I spend most days working the tills and sorting out stock. This means that I have to spend a lot of time communicating with customers. To begin with I was quite excited to start working. I thought it would be a good opportunity to work on my social skills and maybe overcome my anxiety issues. Over the course of this time, my boss has commented multiple times on my poor communication skills and is getting frustrated with my inability to function like a <<normal human being>>. I often suffer the infamous mind blanks when being instructed to do something, and usually have to ask people to repeat themselves. I struggle to be polite to customers and often mumble and mutter under my breath. I've most certainly become more comfortable with social situations since starting but I'm finding it harder and harder to muster the enthusiasm to go into work each day. Since starting, I've become very depressed and am considering leaving. Everyone I work with thinks I'm an idiot. I constantly make mistakes due to my anxiety issues. My mind is so pre-occupied with feeling anxious that it's difficult to focus on anything else."

That's the main issue when you're dealing with social anxiety: you spend all your energy trying to appear "normal" instead of focusing on your tasks.

At my first job, I used to literally collapse at the end of the work day, because I was mentally exhausted. I've already told you about my string of unsuccessful job interviews, and my work-related issues didn't stop there. Attending networking events or business gatherings, speaking up during meetings, socializing with my coworkers during breaks – all was incredibly difficult in the beginning. I was dreading the fact that I needed to go to work and spent my days feeling incompetent. Also, I was under the impression that my coworkers were waiting for me to fail so that they could point out my mistakes and make fun of me. At one point, I even became paranoid that one of my colleagues was keeping track of how often I visited the restroom, so that he could tease me about this later on. I didn't feel like I would ever be able to fit in.

This is another common issue people dealing with social phobia experience – the burden of feeling like they don't belong. "I feel like the most awkward coworker. I don't know how to socialize with fellow colleagues (...). I can do my job well except for the speaking part and that's basically a trait that a career must have. I look hostile, snobbish, moody, timid in front of everyone. I know that colleagues talk about me and that worsens my anxiety more", another user wrote on the forum.

Performance reviews are dreaded by everyone, but they become surreal nightmares for people with social anxiety: "If I make a mistake at work and I am corrected on that, I think about it constantly and wonder if I have made the same mistake before and obsess about it. I hate it and it causes so much anxiety. I know that I am a hard worker and good at my job, but those mistakes really get to me. I guess I am just afraid of being judged at all even though I am more harsh on myself than anyone else."

Last, but not least, social phobia can prevent you from sharing your ideas with your colleagues and supervisors. It can be crippling just thinking about how it will be to hold a presentation in front of your colleagues or explain a report or plan you came up with to your manager. The fear of interaction can prevent you from being proactive at work; and can cause you to pass up professional opportunities.

At the end of the day, the ugly truth is that your relationship with colleagues and managers weighs a lot when it's time for a raise or promotion. That hiring managers are looking for people who would fit in with the team. That you must network if you're looking to climb the career ladder. And you won't be able to get far if you can't keep your anxiety in check.

The Most Common Workplace Anxieties

Everyone faces some level of workplace-related anxiety. For people dealing with social phobia though, this anxiety often leads to obsessive worrying or avoidance. When you have social phobia, you can dread waking up in the morning to go into the office, and seemingly mundane activities like breaks or company events become a source of continuous stress.

People with social anxiety don't fret only over how they will get their assignments done or interact with clients; more often than not, they can be overly concerned with how they will greet their coworkers in the morning or how they can plan their breaks so they don't have to make small talk during the day. What to the regular folk seems extreme becomes routine to the socially anxious.

While there are many situations that can make people who have social phobia overly worry, here are the most common anxieties that cause their pulses to race in offices everywhere.

Job interviews

It's not easy to get a job when you have social anxiety. Making a good impression during an interview is difficult when you're constantly sweating. Plus, the fear of making a fool of yourself or getting rejected can easily keep you from even trying.

Speaking up during a meeting

Whether you're expected to hold a presentation or you simply want to share a few ideas with the group, speaking up to a crowd is intimidating, to say the least. There's no wonder public speaking is the number one fear most Americans share, ranking higher than death. Speaking up during a meeting can make people with social phobia panic in a heartbeat; mainly because they feel embarrassed to express their opinions or be singled out in front of colleagues. This applies to conference calls as well. Plus, when you're dealing with social anxiety, this fear can also make you turn down jobs or promotions that can bring you one step closer to the career you always dreamed about.

Remembering people's names

I am never able to remember someone's name after only hearing it once. When you deal with clients on a regular basis, this can quickly become an issue. Furthermore, while a regular individual doesn't generally feel ashamed to ask the new acquaintance to repeat the name, people with social anxiety often end up obsessing over the issue. They beat themselves up because of their "incompetence," which only makes them feel more inadequate and insecure.

Eating in front of others

When you are dealing with social anxiety, eating in front of others becomes a hassle. You worry excessively about looking like a slob when chewing or handling food in front of coworkers. For the first months at my first job I wasn't able to enjoy one single bite of the lunch I used to pack from home. I felt like everyone's eyes were pointed at me, waiting for me to do something completely ungracious. I ended up eating only yogurt for lunch, because there was a relatively smaller chance I could screw that up.

Using the restroom

Public restrooms are places of nightmares for people with social anxiety. There is such thing as shy bladder syndrome, and it's not fun to experience. Neither is spying on the restroom door until you are positive that there's no one else in there.

Interacting with coworkers

Everything from small talk to meetings becomes almost unbearable when you're dealing with social phobia. You're often under the impression that everyone thinks you are unskilled and have no business working there. As one of the users of the forum I mentioned in the previous chapter puts it: "I feel my co-workers watching me to see when I have made a mistake. They can't wait to be the one to point out how I screwed up and report it as though the building has been set on fire. I have an overwhelming sense of panic when I know I am being watched and talked about as though I am the only one making mistakes". Plus, if you are attracted to a colleague, things get even worse. I, for one, used to constantly worry about even the sheer possibility of workplace attraction.

Dealing with supervisors

Regular meetings with your supervisors can become manageable; but when you're called in unexpectedly or the manager comes by to ask you a question, panic and distress quickly set in. Two big categories of workplace anxiety are perfectionism and fear of interacting with authority figures. A supervisor asking for a meeting can trigger both. Simply running into the CEO in the hallway or elevator can be a source or anxiety. Should you say "Hello?" Should you make small talk? Do you look alright? These encounters can cripple you with self-doubt.

Company social events

Company social events can also become anxiety triggers. While others seem to relax and enjoy themselves, someone with social phobia will worry about what would happen if they were left standing alone; or what would it be like if they don't know what to say when they are approached by someone with whom they don't interact on a regular basis. A user of the social anxiety forum accurately describes these types of situations: "Today my boss took my group at work out for our quarterly luncheon. It's a nice gesture to thank everyone for their hard work. Everyone (except me) had a good time laughing and joking with one another. Like many times before, I may have said two words the entire time. I sat quietly, with a stupid look on my face trying to act as though I fit in, when actually if I could have run out the door, I would have. I squirmed in my seat feeling so uncomfortable and inadequate waiting for the moment to leave. It was unbearable".

Interacting with clients

Dealing with clients can be exhausting for someone with social phobia. Another user of the social anxiety forum explains how they were transferred because of their disorder: "My position is supposed to be a marketing/customer service position and I have to work in our clients' offices to show how much our company cares for them; but it just makes my social anxiety worse, because now I feel like when I'm around people I have to put in the extra effort to please them. However, that pressure, as you know, only works opposite. So, after being pushed from client to client office, I'm being moved back to our admin office. It sounds great, but I still feel like a failure".

There are other more minor anxieties workers have to deal with: fear that they will be dressed inappropriately, that they won't be able to keep up with technology, or that they will make a mistake and everyone will notice. Many even avoid asking any types of questions because they are worried they would seem incompetent. It's not easy to work with people when you have social anxiety, that's for sure. If you take it one day at a time, however, and come up with ways to make you cope better, it will become manageable over time.

General Advice to Keep Social Anxiety in Check

There are several general strategies that anyone can use to manage their anxiety. While the results won't happen overnight, being persistent can significantly improve your quality of life. Learning how to relax, working on your self-confidence, and taking better care of yourself are all steps in the right direction. Here are a few things you should try.

Take care of yourself

This should be rule number one for everyone. There's a good chance that your anxiety becomes worse when you don't get enough sleep or when you have too much on your plate. To live a fulfilling and less stressful existence you will need to pace yourself. Make sure you sleep at least 7-8 hours every night, embrace a healthier diet, and exercise regularly. Also, limit alcohol and caffeine, since these substances can aggravate anxiety and trigger panic attacks. You will feel better and more confident.

On the same note, remember to be kind to yourself. Set aside enough time every day to regroup and relax, don't take on more projects than you can handle, and make time to see those special people in your life who offer support or understanding. Tell friends and family when you're overwhelmed and let them know how they can be of assistance.

Work on your confidence

Since social phobia is often linked to low self-esteem, work on improving your self-confidence. The better you feel about yourself, the less inadequate you will feel in front of others. Start by making a list of all your qualities and accomplishments and carry it with you at all times. Whenever you feel low, glance over it and remember how awe-inspiring you actually are. Next, stop comparing yourself to others. You should only be in competition with yourself, not with those around you. Analyze how much you've grown in the last few years and be proud of all your successes, big or small.

In order to boost your self-esteem, you will also have to adjust your expectations. When these expectations are unrealistic, you're just setting yourself up for failure. Set smaller, short-term goals for yourself instead of long-term ones that are extremely difficult to accomplish. Celebrate each achievement as you move forward and recognize all the hard work you've put into making those small dreams come true.

Challenge your thoughts

When we are anxious, we tend to see everything as threatening and dangerous. We realize deep down that our fears aren't anchored in reality, but we're somehow unable to get rid of them. One strategy that can help with this is to replace anxious thoughts with realistic thoughts. You need to learn how to see things in a clear and fair way, without focusing solely on the bad. Analyze the way you talk to yourself and try to replace negative statements with realistic ones. This involves looking at all aspects of a given situation - the positive, the negative, and the neutral - before making conclusions.

For example, let's say you need to go to your friend's birthday party. That usually means stressing over who else will be there and how it would be best to interact with them. Instead of thinking that "the party will be horrible, no one will talk to me and I will make a fool of myself," (negative), consider what could go right. Maybe the party will be boring or uneventful (neutral), or maybe you will meet some interesting people and even strike up some fun conversations (positive). Force yourself to see the whole picture. It will take some time to switch your thinking process, so be patient and practice.

Learn to relax

When you're dealing with social anxiety, it feels like at any moment you are surely going to say or do the wrong thing in public, in front of people who know you. To lessen that fear you need to learn how to relax. Set aside some time during the day to wind down and recharge. Try meditation or yoga – both great practices that help you stay calm and focused, but well-known for their ability to reduce stress.

Additionally, find other activities that bring you joy and peace of mind during the day: like listening to a fun podcast on your way to work, having lunch with a close friend you're comfortable with, drawing yourself a warm bath after a long day. All these relaxing activities will have a positive impact on your social anxiety.

Breathe

Calm breathing can be a socially anxious person's best friend. Whenever you feel overly stressed or anxious, focusing on your breathing can help you regain your calm. When anxiety strikes, it often causes you to breathe faster, which can then make you feel dizzy or even more self-conscious and stressed. Calm breathing involves taking slow and gentle breaths.

The practice is fairly simple: breathe in through the nose, pause, and then breathe out through the mouth, pausing for several seconds before taking another breath. Around six to eight such breathing cycles per minute should be enough to decrease your anxiety and help you take the edge off.

Finally, it's important not to try to suppress your anxiety. At the end of the day, it's not a willpower issue. Your aim should be to learn how to cope with it. Don't try to make it go away, since it's unrealistic. Think about it: if it were possible, no one would have to deal with the disorder anymore. Embrace social anxiety as a part of who you are and strive to develop strategies that will help you minimize it. Once you figure out what strategies work for you, it will be that much easier to keep your anxious feelings in check.

Part 2 – Coping With Social Anxiety in Your Professional Life

How to Cope With Job Interview Anxiety

Job interviews can cause a bit of anxiety for everyone. If you're dealing with social phobia though, they can be downright terrifying. One member of the social anxiety support forum I've mentioned previously was kind enough to share such a horrible experience: "When I was invited to come into their office for a face to face interview I actually took a sleeping pill before I left the house because that was the only thing I had available to prevent me freaking out with nerves. I was mortified when I arrived there and not one but two women called me into an empty interview room. Both of them looking at me, I felt very sick as I walked in and took my seat. As I am not around people that much in everyday life I knew I would miss a lot of normal social cues and how to even behave. Frankly, I cannot remember much of what I said but I could detect a hint of sarcasm in their tone of voice because it probably was obvious to them how uncomfortable I was. It was so scary answering their questions and even having to tell not such accurate descriptions about my previous job experience just to get a better chance at getting a job. I think they really had a good laugh after I left there". When you're experiencing regular levels of anxiety, you can eventually manage to fake the confidence interviewers are so eagerly looking for, especially with a certain degree of practice. When you're socially anxious, you feel the need to resort to extreme measures to calm your nerves – hence the sleeping pill.

For people with social phobia, job interviews are not only anxiety-provoking, but almost impossible to get through. You are required to meet strangers who are basically in a position of authority, and you need to talk about yourself and your accomplishments. They then proceed to judge you based not only on your answers, but your appearance and overall demeanor as well. These aren't good odds for those who find it hard just to interact with others on a daily basis. In extreme cases, talking to a therapist and getting treatment is necessary to get you through tough situations like this. However, there are also a few strategies you can try to calm your nerves and make a better first impression. Here are a few ideas.

Treat yourself well

Again, I can't emphasize how important this is. Make sure you get a good night's sleep and eat a nutritious breakfast before heading out the door. If possible, get some exercise or meditate for a bit in the morning. This could greatly contribute to your success, since they are both practices known for their stress lowering abilities. In short, focus on engaging in activities that you know boost your confidence and calm you down. Also, avoid caffeine and alcohol.

Prepare

To reduce job interview anxiety, eliminate any other stressors that are unrelated to the actual meeting.

Examples include getting lost, uncomfortable clothing, or showing up late. Pick an appropriate outfit beforehand, one you know fits well and makes you look professional. The shoes should be comfortable as well. If you're a woman, don't stress over putting on too much make-up or showing up with a fancy hairdo – a simpler look works better anyway. A touch of blush and mascara, a quick up-do and you can be on your way.

If you are unfamiliar with the location of the interview, scout the building in advance. Give yourself plenty of time to get to know the area and maybe even do a trial run the day before, to see how long it takes you to get there and make sure you will be able to make it to the interview on time.

Do your homework

Every bit of preparation you can do will significantly increase your comfort level, so go out of your way when researching the employer. Find out everything you can about the company and the position you're applying for. Follow the company on social networks to get a better sense of what they are looking for and figure out how the ambiance at the office is. Make a list of potential interview questions and come up with answers for each one. Don't forget about the specifics of the job as well. You should be ready to list your accomplishments, tell the employer why you're a good fit for the job, and highlight your skills. You can find a list of common questions asked during job interviews here. All this preparation will help you feel more confident and capable during the interview.

Rehearse

This might sound silly, but rehearsing before the big day will also lower your overall stress and anxiety. Ask a friend or loved one to sit down with you and go through all the interview questions, one by one. Wear the outfit you've already picked out and make the whole "mock interview" seem as real as possible.

Visualize success

Visualization is much more than positive thinking – it actually gets your brain ready to behave in the way you desire. For it to work, however, it must be done correctly. Before the big meeting, find a quiet space where you won't be disturbed and take a few deep breaths. When you're ready, close your eyes and then visualize yourself being successful at your interview. For more information on how visualization works, you can take a look here.

Take your time

Remember that the interview isn't a sprint, it's a marathon. No one is rushing you. Accept a glass of water from the interviewer and take a few sips whenever you feel pressured. It's better to take your time before coming up with an answer instead of blurting out the first thing that comes through your head. Also, keep in mind that an interview is a two-way street. A great way to take the pressure off you is to ask the employer a few questions. In fact, it's highly recommended, since the whole interview should look more as a conversation rather than an overly uptight formal discussion.

Once it's all over, no matter how the interview goes, congratulate yourself as you step out the door. Pat yourself on the back. Buy yourself a treat. Don't obsess over how it could have gone better. You had the guts to face your fear and take your chances. You deserve a small celebration.

How to Successfully Handle Meetings

Oh, the dreaded work meetings! Not only are they widely known to decrease workers' productivity in office environments worldwide, they can also become extreme stressors for people who suffer from social phobia. They can even cause you to miss out on a promotion because you were too anxious to speak up during a meeting. Or maybe you declined a promotion altogether because it would have meant conducting these gatherings yourself. Believe me, I've been there.

Personally, I used to barely speak a word during the first couple of months at my first office job. I felt like everyone was staring at me, eagerly waiting for me to say something stupid and make a fool of myself. I only later found out that my direct supervisor was actually hoping I'd speak up more often, because I was able to make a few good points once I got a chance to properly express myself – most often via email. As I got more comfortable and practiced my presentation skills more, I began to slowly overcome my meeting-related anxiety. It also helped that I was blessed with a few wonderful coworkers who were there for me during those horrible first months, believing in my talent and providing support and encouragement on a regular basis.

During those stressful times I managed to pick up a few tricks on how to lessen my anxiety during business meetings. Here are a few ideas that might help you as well.

Accept your anxiety

We perform at our peak when we're able to focus on the task at hand, without any distractions. When you're suffering from social anxiety though, it claims the best of you. You feel the anxiety and focus on controlling it, which only increases the tension even more. Thereby, you try even harder to contain yourself. It's a vicious cycle.

Here's another approach: relinquish control.

Stop stressing over the fact that you're anxious. Notice your anxiety and accept that this is normal for you. It's there. You're overly familiar with it. Once this is acknowledged, you will have a better chance of focusing on what's actually going on in the meeting. Do your best to see these unsettling feelings like simple bumps in the road instead of giving them the power to become an insurmountable hurdle. This way you manage to lower their significance, consequently allowing them less control over your behavior.

Prepare

If you are expected to present during a meeting, do all the hard work before it's time to speak up in front of everybody. Write your presentation and rehearse it exhaustively. Use plenty of visual aids and notes to feel more comfortable during the meeting.

Additionally, consider joining a group like Toastmasters to improve your public speaking skills. Just the idea of joining such a group can be frightening, I know, but the benefits are worth it big time. You will have the chance to become better at making introductions, thinking on your feet, and talking in front of other people. Plus, during the first few sessions you only observe – if you do decide that this is too much to handle, you don't have to go through with it.

Get there early

You might feel tempted to join your co-workers last-minute, so you're not required to interact with anyone before the meeting begins. That's not such a good idea. By arriving five minutes early, you get the chance to accommodate with the group and ease into the conversation. To feel more relaxed, consider calling a friend or loved one for a few minutes before stepping in – you may be able to carry this composed state into the meeting; at the very least, you will hopefully feel less tense and awkward. Pick a spot where you feel comfortable in and greet people with a smile as they arrive. This makes you look friendlier and less hostile.

Trust your strengths

If you're dealing with social phobia, you might never become the most eloquent speaker in the group. And that's OK. However, that doesn't mean that you can't use your strengths to your advantage. Your listening skills are your best friend – use them confidently whenever someone else has the table and then choose your words with care when it's your turn to speak up. People may not consider you as a very spontaneous colleague, but they will surely value your patience and wisdom.

Also, learn as much as you can about the meeting's agenda in advance and research possible topics that may come up, to boost your confidence. Unfortunately, you will also have to prepare yourself to respond to unexpected questions and discuss issues that aren't pre-planned. The key here is to not let your anxiety take over when you realize that you don't have an answer prepared. Typically, it's perfectly OK to admit that you are unsure about something and to say that you will look into it and get back to everybody later on.

"I have extreme anxiety when it comes to business meetings. I sit there wondering if they can tell I am screaming inside to just get the hell out of the room," another member of the social anxiety forum wrote. If you're in the same boat, there are two things you must keep in mind: you're not alone, and there are ways to get better. You won't be able to improve without practice though, so it's time to get out of your comfort zone.

Networking with Social Anxiety

Most people have some level of social anxiety, especially when it comes to making new connections. Fear of embarrassment or rejection can easily trump the thrilling urge to meet a new business partner, future employer, or sales prospect. Making the first move can bring on everything from tense muscles to a racing heart. And when you suffer from social phobia, networking events can be downright frightening.

Unfortunately for those of us who are socially anxious, networking has become mandatory in today's competitive job market. More often than not, getting your dream job is less a matter or what you know and more a matter of who you know. Having someone to vouch for you when you send in an application for a new gig can make a huge difference for the hiring manager; consequently, establishing and nurturing professional relationships should be one of your priorities.

But how can you pull that off when the sole thought of sharing a room with a plethora of strangers makes you sweat profusely? Again, the secret lies in preparation. The more familiar you get with the event at hand and the guest list, the less panicked you will feel once the big day arrives and you're required to mingle with a bunch of strangers. Here are some tips that tremendously helped me along the way.

Do some research

Before you attend the event, take a look on the event's website to find out more about the location, agenda, and guest list. The more you learn about the circumstances you will find yourself in, the more comfortable you will feel. If we're talking about a more informal or low-scale gathering, talk to the organizers and ask for more details. It's important to know who's going to be there and what subjects will be covered during presentations.

Getting prepared for the big day should also be on your to-do list. Remember when we talked about how useful it is to eliminate stressors that are unrelated to the actual meeting before a job interview? The same goes here. Pick a comfortable outfit, get familiar with the location of the event beforehand, and avoid substances like caffeine and alcohol.

Realize it's about quality, not volume

Before you embark on your networking adventure, keep this in mind: more often than not, it's not important to connect with a lot of people. It's important to connect with the right people. Peruse the guest list and determine who would be most beneficial to interact with, depending on your career goals. Maybe an executive from the company you want to work for will be there; or maybe you can interact with someone who could sponsor your startup idea. Focus on establishing connections only with people who can truly help you advance your career and ignore the rest of the crowd.

This can go a long way when it comes to reducing your anxiety. Set a certain goal for each networking event in particular (like interacting with X or handing your business card to Y) and direct all your strength towards reaching that objective. You don't need to waste your energy making small talk with everybody in the room.

Reach out on social media

Once you figure out who the key players you wish to connect with are, find them on social media prior to the networking event. Engaging people first through social networks can help you make the transition to real life interactions easier. It sets up a certain comfort level that will come in handy when it's time for face to face interactions. You can send them a message on Twitter or LinkedIn and introduce yourself. Explain that you're going to attend the event as well and that you're looking forward to exchanging a few words as soon as you get the chance.

This strategy is pretty great – once you engage with those people in real life, they will already know who you are and you can cut short the amount of time wasted on introductions. Get straight to the point and skip the small talk part. There's a good chance you will make a good impression as well, since this approach shows that you don't want to waste their time and you value efficiency. In short, you have nothing to lose.

Rehearse your introduction

Regardless of your preparation skills, unexpected situations arise all the time. Someone might want to introduce you to someone else, or someone might come up to you and engage in a conversation. You will be much better equipped to handle these types of situations if you rehearse a few short phrases that help you introduce yourself. You can practice with a friend or loved one to make things easier. State your name, occupation, and the company you work for.

Also, it's a good idea to prepare a few topics to bring up during casual conversations. Recent developments in the industry, new technologies, upcoming trends – these kinds of subjects are generally well received by a professional audience. They will make you appear well-informed and prepared; plus, having something to talk about can go a long way when it comes to decreasing your anxiety levels.

Direct the attention on other people

A lot of the stress and tension associated with networking relates to the concern that you will have to talk excessively about yourself. That doesn't have to be the case. A better approach is to think about what you can find out about the people you wish to connect with. Prepare a few interesting questions to ask during the conversation. You will get to know the other person better and shift the focus from yourself.

A good idea is to use questions that start with "why" and "how" instead of "what" and "where." Asking someone "What do you do?" generally leads to a brief answer. Asking them "Why did your company decide to do x?" or "Why did you decide to attend this event?" are more likely to break the awkwardness and help you ignite an engaging conversation.

Networking can be extremely difficult when you're dealing with social phobia. However, it's important to be willing to force yourself to experience these types of uncomfortable social situations if you're looking to climb the corporate ladder. Practice makes perfect, so get out there and deal with your issues hands on. The tips above should help you considerably lessen your anxiety.

Be kind to yourself though. If the event suddenly gets too much to handle, take a break or leave. Having a full-on panic attack in the middle of a crowd is not something you will remember fondly later on. Accept your short-comings, but do your best to overcome them whenever you get the chance. As painful as networking can be, missing out on great professional opportunities because of your phobia is much worse.

How to Calmly Deal with Clients

Some aspects of work itself can be challenging for those with social anxiety. Meetings were a good example; cold calling clients or interacting with them face-to-face is another. Ideally, when you suffer from social phobia, it's best to pick a career in which communicating with others isn't a big aspect of the job. It's important to get out there and socialize, but overwhelming yourself on a regular basis can be counterintuitive.

Unfortunately, not all of us can afford that luxury. When dealing with clients is part of your job description, you will need to dodge a lot of anxiety triggers on a daily basis. If you're not careful, the combination of negative self-evaluations and potential negative reactions from clients can be a recipe for disaster. Here are a few ideas of what you can do to cope better with your day-to-day responsibilities.

Develop a manageable routine

When you're required to socialize on the job, take your mornings and evenings to unwind and recharge. Don't schedule any stressful interactions after work, and reserve your mornings to mentally prepare for what's to come. Taking up yoga or meditation can help – a quick session each morning will considerably lower your stress levels. In the evenings, try a relaxing bath or lose yourself in a good book to recover.

Outline scenarios

Coming up with different scripts you can recite when interacting with clients isn't such a good idea. Usually, the person on the other end of the conversation can tell if you're reading from a script, and you risk coming across as less genuine. Plus, reciting something you previously memorized detaches you from the content and allows your mind to wonder. If the client interrupts you abruptly, it will be harder to get the conversation back on track.

However, you should take the time to create a general outline you can refer to, in order to boost your comfort level. Think of a few ideas for subjects to bring up during the interaction and come up with a few lines you can use, depending on the scenario at hand. Also, make sure that you know both the name of the client you need to interact with and how you're supposed to pronounce it. The more prepared you are, the less anxious you will feel.

As a side note, it's also wise to practice what you are going to say. Record yourself speaking and make changes based on what you hear. If you don't think you can be objective enough, ask a loved one to give you feedback. They can also help you practice these conversations in advance.

Fake it

Did you ever hear the phrase "fake it 'til you make it?" It works. As long as you have the time to properly prepare, there's no reason why things shouldn't work out in your favor. Sit straight as you talk, put a smile on your face, and do your best to speak with confidence. Eventually, as you gain more experience with these interactions, your anxiety will decrease. Take it one step at a time.

I read a great piece of advice on the social anxiety support forum I've previously mentioned. One user was complaining about the fact that they had to deal with a rude customer, and how it was difficult not to let the client's bad behavior influence them for the worst. Another one responded with the following: "You just gotta remember not to take that stuff personal. This may sound weird, but when I have to deal with someone that arrogant, the chorus from that old Jimmy Buffet song starts going off in my head and it makes me smile. The verse is 'were you born an ******* or did you work at it your whole life? Either way it worked out fine because you're an ******* tonight!' It actually does make'em easier to deal with because I start looking at them as if they were a 12 year old throwing a temper tantrum. It's a good reminder that some people just enjoy being a jerk and you can't give them the satisfaction of letting it get under your skin." True story.

Take regular breaks

Taking breaks during your work day is important; if you're suffering from social phobia and are required to constantly interact with others, even more so. Short breaks help you ease the tension, release stress, and stay alert. Consider taking a short walk, grabbing a snack, or spending a few minutes in the break room, to allow your mind to refocus. On the same note, don't skip your lunch break. Instead, use it as an opportunity to get some much-needed alone time. You can grab a sandwich and go to a nearby park or a café to regroup.

Take notes

I'm a big fan of taking notes during a conversation with a client. I find that it's a great way to avoid slipping into negative thought patterns, because you can focus better on what the other person is saying. Additionally, you will have a written record of what was discussed that you can refer to during future conversations or use later on to improve your skills.

If interacting with clients is within your job duties, try to keep a positive attitude and push through the rough patches. Remember that there is no such thing as a perfect interaction and that we're all human. Even if you slip up during a conversation and say the wrong thing, there's a small chance the other person will take it personally. Focus on doing the best job you can and remember to take regular breaks to avoid feeling overwhelmed and ever more panicky.

How to Manage Office Crushes

We all know the downsides of dating a coworker. However, when you develop a crush on someone at work, all your worries can easily fall by the wayside. Emotions become impossible to ignore, while that rational voice in your head keeps getting quieter. After all, you see this person every day, in their element, being good at what they do. It's tempting to throw caution in the wind and follow your feelings.

When you have social phobia, things are a bit different. Instead of getting excited by the possibility of making it work with your office crush, you start to get incredibly flustered whenever they're around. Your ability to speak coherently is affected, you're worried of looking like a fool, and your fear of rejection can easily drive you crazy. When I had my first office crush, I was seriously tempted to quit just so I wouldn't be forced to interact with that person on a daily basis. My crush was only bringing additional stress into my life, and that stress was excruciatingly hard to handle. Acting on my feelings wasn't even a possibility, as my low self-esteem could hardly allow me to make small talk with the colleague in question. Those were the dark times.

As I've spent most of my life in office environments though, I've learned that the occasional crush is unavoidable. It's easy to develop certain feelings for someone with whom you're working closely; the trick for getting through the day is to remember (1) that those feelings don't control you and (2) that "feeling" isn't the same as "acting". It's OK to like someone—anyone. But liking someone doesn't always mean that you're required to act on those feelings. I found this realization to be extremely liberating. Once I understood that I don't have to allow my feelings to dictate my actions, it was much easier to keep them under control.

If you're worried about how you crush affects your work performance, here are a few ideas that might help.

Keep things professional

Above all else, make sure you stay professional in the workplace. Avoid any unprofessional behavior that you crush may cause: calling in sick repeatedly just to avoid dealing with them, taking long lunches on a regular basis, not finishing your assignments on time because you've spent the last two hours trying to come up with something to say the next time you see them. Otherwise, things can get very bad, very quickly. Maintaining contact limited to professional issues will help you keep things in perspective. Not to mention ensure that you keep your job.

Perform regular reality checks

When you have a crush on someone, it's not uncommon to let the thoughts about that person become the main focus of your day. Don't. Keep your feet firmly rooted in reality. Always remember that you're stronger than your feelings, that you shouldn't feel guilty because you like someone, and that you mustn't allow your fondness to dictate your behavior. Your crush may take advantage of your weakness for them and try to walk all over you at the office in order to get ahead. Don't allow them to. Keep focusing on your assignments instead of letting your thoughts wonder aimlessly. You need to act as calm and collected as possible.

Keep your feelings private

Do not share your feelings about your workplace crush with anyone at the office; otherwise things may get extremely uncomfortable. I also strongly advise against sharing your emotions with the object of your affection as well. If you do decide to act on those feelings, start by sending clear signals and see how the crush reacts. If you confess your endless love and they don't feel the same way, it's unfair to them and potentially embarrassing to you.

Set clear boundaries for yourself

Setting safe boundaries will make coping much easier. Intimacy doesn't occur in the presence of others, so do your best to design strategies that remove private contact with your crush. As much as possible, only interact with them when there are other people around. Also, respect the other person's personal space. Don't sneak up to their cubicle unannounced or "accidentally" bump into them in the break room. Not only is this type of behavior juvenile, the sole planning of these interactions will require a lot of energy from your part and can easily boost your anxiety levels.

Check the office policy

Some companies expressly discourage office romances. Browse through the employee manual to determine if that's the case. If you find you that co-workers are prohibited from dating, this can be incentive enough to keep your feelings in check and act professionally. When that's not the case, think about the consequences. Remember that job security is more important than fleeting feelings and that you are there to earn a paycheck, not mingle with your colleagues.

Having a crush on someone at work can bring additional and unnecessary stress into your already-filled-with-anxiety life. More often than not, acting on your feelings isn't worth it, so do your best to keep them in check. Sure, there are numerous stories of people who met their significant other at work and lived happily ever after. But that's because people are less likely to talk about the embarrassing failures they had to endure when dating a coworker. Keep your feelings in check and act professional. Your affection will dial down with time.

How to Ask for a Promotion/Raise

Asking for a raise or promotion is challenging, to say the least. You're required to talk about yourself and highlight your accomplishments, plead for your case, and be able to point out all the reasons why you're a valuable asset for the company. Meetings with authority figures are stressful as it is; and asking for recognition generally isn't a favorite pass-time activity for people with social anxiety. If you want to get ahead in the workplace though, you need to prepare for these interactions and learn how to successfully sell yourself.

Before you ask for a meeting with your direct supervisor, it's important to know the worth of your job. Try a few salary comparison websites and determine if you're underpaid. Also, look for a way to qualify all the good work you've been doing. Are your projects going well? Did you put in any extra time lately? Having solid arguments to present to your employer is crucial. Plus, asking for a raise simply because you feel like you've been with the company for a while isn't wise. A raise means something extra, and you need to prove that you deserve it.

If you think about it, asking for a raise isn't that much different than a job interview. The only thing that's changes is that your supervisor had enough time to figure out how skilled and valuable you are, so chances of things going in your favor are actually higher. Here are a few things you should try in order to ease the anxiety associated with asking for a promotion.

Pick your timing wisely

Sometimes, timing is everything, especially in the office. Ideally, you should ask for a salary bump after you've completed a difficult project, solved an issue the company was struggling with, or taken on new responsibilities. In short: after you've done something notable. Another way to go is to wait for a performance review – this way, your boss is more familiar with your recent accomplishments.

Whatever you do, don't pick a day when your manager seems moody or irritable. If the company is going through a rough patch (if there were recent layoffs, for instance), it's also best to avoid the subject. Check the employee manual as well – if the company's standard is to offer employees only one salary bump per year, asking for more money any other time isn't recommended.

Make a list of accomplishments

Asking for a promotion will be a much more comfortable experience if you're well prepared. A good idea is to put together a small presentation that explains why you deserve a salary bump. Visual aids are usually handy when it comes to easing social anxiety. Include specific examples of your performance, or use a slideshow presentation to hit your highlights during the time you spent with the company thus far. Be as specific and detail-oriented as possible. Mention projects that went well, problems you solved for the business along the way, duties you handled gracefully.

If you're not planning to use any kind of visual aids, at least write down a few key points you need to hit while pleading your case. Rehearsing your presentation is also wise. Again, you can practice in front of a mirror or ask a loved one to help.

Don't whine

Whining won't win you any bonus points. Don't go into your supervisor's office and start complaining about your workload or about how undervalued you feel. Instead, focus on emphasizing your results. Also, whatever you do, don't talk about your personal issues. Your supervisor isn't your friend and they shouldn't care that you're currently going through a rough patch – like if your car broke down or if you overdrew your personal checking account and don't have any savings to rely on. A raise or promotion should be based solely on merit. Keep it professional and only talk about your achievements and capability.

Bringing up your anxiety issues during the meeting is also unadvisable, regardless of any progress you might have made during the time you've worked for the company. A lot of people ask me if they should tell their employer about their social phobia and I always tell them the same thing: it's up to you. Some people want to keep it hidden and work on their issues on their own, while others want to educate people about their condition or need special accommodations. Whatever the case, you should avoid being defined by your anxiety. Earning a raise should be based on your professional achievements only, so steer the conversation away from how hard you had to work to overcome your anxiety issues. If your employer is familiar with your condition, they can appreciate your efforts and dedication even if you don't point them out.

Keep calm

Things may not go your way, so acknowledge that this is a possibility before diving in. If your boss's answer to your request for a raise is negative, don't panic. It's important to prepare for this possibility as well, so have a back-up plan in place. For example, you can ask them exactly what areas you should work on to improve yourself, or what you can do to qualify for a salary bump later on.

A lot of people threaten to quit when this happens, but be aware: this is dangerous territory. No one likes ultimatums, and your employer might take your stand as a sign of disloyalty. Make sure you have another serious offer available before resorting to this bold approach. If your supervisor takes you up on that and you don't follow through, it's unlikely they will take you seriously ever again.

As you can see, it's all about preparation. When you know exactly what you're going to say and what achievements you need to highlight, your stress levels significantly decrease. You will dazzle your boss with your strengths instead of exposing your flaws. The important thing is to stay positive. With the right attitude, you will be climbing up the ladder in no time.

Quick Relaxation Techniques That Work

Workdays can get hectic. Despite your preparation and coping mechanisms, they can still become overwhelming. Your supervisor has a bad day and lashes out at you, or maybe one of your colleagues is way chattier than usual. When your day gets too chaotic, you need to quickly calm yourself down to avoid your anxiety from escalating. Luckily, there are a few effective relaxation techniques that actually work. Here are a few examples.

Take deep breaths

We already talked about deep breathing in part one of this book, but it's a practice worth mentioning again, especially since it's extremely efficient and doesn't require much time. Sit up straight, close your eyes, and put a hand on your belly. Gradually inhale through your nose, feel the breath start in your abdomen and work its way up. You will feel calmer and more able to think clearly in no time.

Be more mindful

When interacting with others becomes overwhelming, take a couple of minutes to notice your surroundings and be more mindful of where you are and how your body is reacting. Notice how your feet are resting on the floor, how your hands shiver, or how your muscles are tense. Focus on your senses and do your best to relieve the tension. When you suddenly become aware of where you are and what you're doing, you have a better chance to slowly evaporate your stress.

Talk to yourself

When you feel anxious negative thoughts tend to pile up. Much of what we say to ourselves when experiencing anxiety can cause us to feel even more anxious. Focus on telling yourself calming phrases such as: "This feeling will pass," "I will get through this," "I am strong and I can handle this," or "I am feeling anxious now, but soon I will be calm." This is called positive self-talk, something us social anxious-types should engage in more often.

Involve your sense of smell

Smelling something relaxing can also calm you down. Next time you feel overly-anxious, rely on aromatherapy. Sniffing calming oils like basil, anise, and chamomile will reduce tension in the body and help increase mental clarity. Keeping a scented candle or some aromatherapy diffuser sticks on your desk should do the trick.

Call a loved one

Hearing a familiar, soothing voice can do wonders when it comes to calming yourself down. Whenever you feel overly stressed or anxious, call a friend or family member and chat for a few minutes. You don't have to vent – simply listening to them tell you about their day can be relaxing. Also, consider using a photo of your loved ones as desktop wallpaper, or place one on your desk. Simply looking at a photo of people you hold dear can be enough to relieve anxiety and feel more in control.

Laugh

In might seem counterintuitive to laugh when you feel anxious, but it will do you a lot of good. Watch a funny video or read some funny comics online. Laughter is known to lower cortisol (the hormone responsible for producing stress) and lighten the load mentally. A few chuckles can improve your mood significantly.

Listen to relaxing tunes

Headphones are your best friends in the workplace, so use them whenever you feel overwhelmed. Listen to nature sounds (the ocean and the sound of birds chirping often have a calming effect); or keep a playlist of all your favorite tunes handy and blast it whenever you feel that your anxiety is getting the best of you. Soothing music lowers blood pressure, heart rate, and anxiety.

Drink tea

Fancy a hot cup of tea? You should. Chamomile tea is extremely popular for its ability to calm the mind and reduce stress. Black tea is also known for keeping stress levels in check and allowing you to concentrate better. Make sure you always have some tea available when you're at the office, just in case things get too hectic.

Stretch

As I've stated before, exercise can significantly decrease stress and anxiety. That being said, going for a run during your lunch break isn't a particularly wise idea, unless you make sure to shower before returning at your desk. However, you can choose the simpler route and only stretch your legs a bit in order to get your blood flowing and give your body a chance to practice dealing with stress. A quick walk around the block or a few stretching exercises in the break room will do the trick and release those much-needed feel-good hormones.

Pet a dog

Surprisingly enough, research has shown that a dog's enthusiasm [can actually be infectious](). Consequently, spending a few quality moments with a pooch can help you feel more relaxed and less burdened by day-to-day worries. Now, I understand that this isn't quite realistic for an office environment; but you can check to see if there aren't any dog parks near your workplace. If that's the case, your lunch break just got that more pleasant.

Use a calming visualization

This technique doesn't even require you to leave your desk. You just need to close your eyes and visualize yourself in a more calming environment. Picture yourself outside, in your favorite park or on a beach somewhere. Watch leaves fly by or notice the clouds passing by in the sky. Assign your anxious thoughts and emotions to these clouds and leaves and watch them float away. You will feel more relieved in a matter of minutes.

Relaxation techniques are a quick way to bring you back into balance. Experiment with different ones and figure out what works best for you. The best part? They only take a few minutes, so you can get back to work in no time.

Conclusion

Dealing with anxiety at the workplace is doable. Keeping your emotions in check is manageable. Interacting with colleagues doesn't have to be terrifying. Most importantly: it's perfectly possible to have a flourishing career even when you suffer from social anxiety. I hope that you found my advice useful and that you're at least a little more optimistic about your professional life than you were before.

This being said, sometimes reaching out to a professional to help you deal with your condition is a must. If you realize that your anxiety is seriously affecting your work life - you can't keep a job or you're miserable at the office - a therapist can provide invaluable insight that will help you cope better. While self-help can go a long way when it comes to lowering your anxiety levels, it's not always enough. If you've tried the techniques and strategies described in this book and you're still struggling with managing your anxiety, you may need professional help as well.

The most effective treatment available for treating social phobia at the moment is cognitive-behavioral therapy (CBT). This type of therapy is based on the premise that what you think affects how you feel, and your feelings affect your behavior. To put it simply, if you can change the way you think about certain social situations that give you anxiety, you will feel much better and function more effectively on a day-to-day basis. CBT usually involves learning how to overcome anxiety triggers by using relaxation techniques and breathing exercises. A therapist can also teach you how to challenge negative thoughts and replace them with more balanced views on the world around you. They will encourage you to face social situations in a systematic way instead of avoiding them all-together.

As time goes by, you will learn how to practice these exercises on your own, and your life will get significantly better. However, until that happens, you may benefit from the extra support and guidance a therapist brings. Remember that there's nothing shameful about asking for help. Quite the opposite.

All in all, no matter how painfully shy you may be and how much you dread everyday interactions, you **can** learn to be comfortable in social situations and reclaim your life. You just need to be willing to take the first step.

Stay Connected

Thanks for reading this book. We hope you found this information helpful and actionable.

You can learn more about ways to improve your relationships from our other books on Amazon, and from our website.

Also, we frequently run special promotions where books in our catalogue are FREE or highly discounted (think $0.99) on Amazon.

We release 1-2 books per month right now – and friends on our list are instantly notified when we make these books free for a few days.

All of our deals are publicized exclusively via our email list.

Join now, and you'll instantly be notified when our freebies happen. Also, you'll get a free copy of our book *The 37 Best Ways to End Conflict in Your Relationships*.

Click the link below to sign up now!

Please visit www.relationshipup.com to join our mailing list and to receive your free gift.

Thank You

Before we part ways for now, we just want to say thank you for purchasing this book and a big congratulations to you for reading it all the way to the end!

There are tons of books out there on relationships, and you decided on this one, and we appreciate it.

If you have any questions, comments, or concerns, you can send an email to us at info@relationshipup.com or visit us on the web. We're always looking to make our books better – so we appreciate ALL feedback!

We'd like to ask for a favor right now – Please take 1 minute and 36 seconds (exactly!) and leave a review for this book on Amazon. Reviews help other people find our books and they help us understand what you liked and what you didn't like about the book – and we want to know what's on your mind so we can do better!

More Books by David Leads

How to Prevent and Manage Sibling Rivalry Among Brothers

How to Practice Empathy: Connect Deeply with Others and Create Meaningful Relationships

9 Ways to Beat Social Anxiety and Shyness: How to Overcome The Fear So You Can Build Meaningful Relationships

Be A Phenomenal Listener: Master the Key to All Effective Communication - Listening

Workplace Anxiety: How to Deal With Stress, Conflict, Toxic Coworkers and Bosses, and Fear of Losing Your Job

Why We're Anxious About Money and How Our Mindset Makes All the Difference

Stay In Love In Marriage: Get Over the Fear of Falling Out of Love

What's Your #1 Fear In Life? Conquering Our 15 Biggest Fears

Get Over It: Put Your Breakup in the Past and Move On

Workplace Bullying: How to Survive and Thrive with a Bully Boss

Printed in Great Britain
by Amazon